Kiss My Curriculum

How to Love Homeschooling and Ignore the Inner Critic

By Rebecca Strömsdörfer

Kiss My Curriculum

Printed in the United States of America

First Printing, 2020

ISBN: 9781708720902

Kindle Direct Publishing

Inquiries should be emailed to rbstroms@gmail.com

Kiss My Curriculum

Dedication

First, I want to thank my husband, my best friend, the man who always believes in me and my abilities, even when I don't believe in myself. He has been my partner in everything. Especially in educating our children. You are my joy and my inspiration. Thank you for being my eternal dreaming and dreamy companion.

To our 5 children Alexa, Ariah, Isaac, Makayla, and Benjamin. You have been a part of my heart since my very existence. You inspire me, you lift me, and you amaze me. I am truly honored to be called your Mother. Thank you for your patience as I learn to be a mother.

Kaylee Larsen, It is because of you that this book was written. You were the one that made me

Kiss My Curriculum

believe that I might have something to share. Thank you for your confidence, your support and especially your editing. You were the one I wrote it to.

Karleen Andresen. My eternal friend. None of this would have been done if it weren't for you. You are my Fairy Godmother who made my dream a reality. You inspire me, push me, and pull things out of me that I didn't even know where there. Thank you for teaching me to be better and reach higher.

Thank you Mom and Dad. You taught me to be feisty, and fight for what was right. You taught me how to speak with God. You helped me keep my compass pointed North. I Love You!

Forward by Sandra Hirst –
My Sister (not a homeschool mom)

Homeschool. Why does this word begin so many passionate, and sometimes heated conversations? Have you ever been in the same room as a public school teacher and a home-school mom as they start to discuss which method is better? It can make you want to cook a big bowl of popcorn and watch the show.

Moms who decide to take it upon themselves to be the main provider of education for their children take on a major challenge, not just to provide daily learning materials to their growing offspring, but they also have to stand up to all the critics around them who "don't approve".

I am married to a public school teacher. I believe that there are phenomenal teachers out there who make a significant impact on the lives of their students. But does that mean every child should go to public school?

Kiss My Curriculum

Sometimes, I am one of those "critics".

Let me introduce you to my sister. We are 1 year apart in age and have the ability to go from insane laughter to a hair-pulling slap fight in less than 5 minutes. We are best friends and worst enemies. She has primarily taught her children at home for the last 16 years. I, on the other hand, literally cried tears of joy the day my youngest started kindergarten. We are absolute opposites, but here is what I have learned from her in the last 16 years.

Home school is insanely difficult. This is not a goal women make on a whim. It takes long discussions, heavy research, and many prayers before a decision is made. I have learned that it is a daily decision that requires incredible sacrifice. I have watched my sister transform much needed living space in her home to a happy and colorful classroom for her five children. She drives them all over town to home-school groups where they learn debate, dance, cello, survival skills, and how to start a business, all

Kiss My Curriculum

while keeping up their math, science, and English studies at home.

I have noticed that home-school moms tend to be deeply religious, and for my sister this also adds church meetings, dinners to neighbors, and babysitting for sick friends. Add her desire to make a difference in the local schools and you now have school board meetings, parent volunteer sign ups, and administration drama.

So many times when I have seen her exhausted I will say "Just put your kids in public school... you just need time to yourself", knowing she will just say something completely noble and loving about the needs of her children coming first. And every time, she has been right. Who knows the needs of their children better than a mother who consults God in all her decisions?

I have watched her 16 and 17 year old daughters turn into talented, amazing, courteous young women who make everyone they talk to feel

Kiss My Curriculum

valued and appreciated. I have watched her 13 year old son build amazing inventions and create successful businesses, who never leaves without giving a hug and mentioning his gratitude for you as a person.

This repentant home-school critic has watched a courageous mother successfully educate her children when the general population told her she couldn't.

I am in awe of all the mothers out there who do what they feel is best for their children regardless of what the masses are pressuring. It is moms like you that are making a difference. I applaud you for your courage.

TABLE OF CONTENTS

Kiss My Curriculum

PREFACE

This book is a memoir – it's about what my husband and I have done as parents to raise confident kids. As each child's confidence grew, I knew I needed to share how we did it, and why.

This is a book about two Christian believers who include God in their daily decisions, and acted on the inspirations received when their kids needed them the most. You'll learn how we educated them, what our worries were and what they were not. Problems we faced and how we solved them. We learned from every situation that came our way.

I'll share those lessons with you in this book. I will be raw, open, honest, and maybe biased. I'm not going to tell you how to raise your kids, but I'll share with you how we raised ours. Hopefully you'll learn from our bad choices (please don't copy those!) and see the humor and attitude that we tend to have in our family.

I want to invite you into our home. It's messy, (but we want it clean). It's humble (but we dream of fancy things). We have great kids, who fight and quarrel one with another and sometimes get on each other's nerves. We love being parents. But we love to be without them sometimes too. We loved having babies but now love sleep-filled nights and dates. This is a real family making real choices and doing real things. Sometimes those choices are not as great as we would like, but we plug along.

Maybe you can take something from us that will help you. Or maybe you will just enjoy poking fun at us. Whatever makes you happy.

This is not a "how-to" book. This is not for philosophers to stew over and analyze. This is not a guilt book or a "parenting dos and don'ts" that will add stress and guilt to your life. I will not tell you what to expect when you are expecting, how to cure "common ailments" (sometimes that's what we call our kids); I am not going to give you the "only" or "best" way to parent.

This book is for the mother who is sitting at home with her first baby and dreams of the amazing wonderful romantic life she will have as she leads this child by the hand to greatness.

This is for the mother who has just had her 3rd child and is feeding that baby with one hand while feeding the toddler the fish crackers and raisins that she hidden in the couch with the other hand, all while hoping that the remaining child doesn't tear apart the house in the meantime.

This is for the mother who wants to find alternative education for her children but doesn't know how and maybe doesn't believe she is capable.

This is for the mother of 8 to 12-year-olds who aren't turning out like she had hoped and is wondering if there is another way.

And this is for the mother who is afraid that teens are messes. That it is only a matter of time before their kids hate them. We especially want to give you hope. Teens are awesome!

Keep in mind, this is not for the skeptic looking for parenting advice. This is not a self-help book, cookbook, or health book.

This is not for the super serious-minded. We don't do serious.

But we do REAL. We do truth.

I am a mother of 5 intensely curious, highly creative, and sometimes overconfident kids (not always a plus by the way). Our children are remarkable! Which shocks us a bit, even though my husband and I have spent the last 20 years praying, studying, and serving over our children so that they might have the best opportunities that God can give them.

I like to think that I have five PhDs – one for each kid. If you calculate the hours I put into parenting my children over the last 20 years, it comes out to be over 200,000 hours of time (and yes, night hours count! It's not like I slept much). That averages to 40,000 hours per child. If 10,000 hours of practice makes you an expert musician, athlete, or artist, then I am an expert - On my kids.

However, do my 200,000 hours make me an expert on your kid? Heck no! But maybe you can take a lesson from my experiences and add it to your own.

That's all I want for you - to glean from this book the parenting, schooling, or life gems that your life or parenting needs to take your life and the lives of your children to the next level. Take what serves you, leave the rest, and find the joy in the mostly mundane adventure that is Parenting.

"A child can teach an adult three things: To be happy for no reason. To always be busy with something. To know how to demand with all his might that which he desires."

-Paulo Coelho

Lesson 1

How I was Homeschooled by my Children

When I first started homeschooling, I was afraid I didn't have what it took to be a homeschool mom (whatever that meant). I was overwhelmed by the amount of curriculum and resources. I knew I didn't have the patience, stamina, or knowledge to do it. There were no classes at the University to teach me how; no PhD I could get so that I could feel confident after I finished my years of study to say I was an expert; no specialty or certificate to gain to say I was qualified.

Kiss My Curriculum

These are all things I was supposed to have before I enter into a life of teaching and inspiring, right? The only qualification I had to homeschool my kids was that I loved them. Is that enough? Well, almost, that, and help from above.

Shocked by that answer? It is because there is one major thing every homeschool parent must have to get through all those fears, rough days, and insecurities. You must hear the call from God. You need to know this is right for your family. Because you will get many, many critics and you have to be able to say, "this is right for us".

You don't choose homeschooling to please the world. Most people just don't get it and that is ok. So join the homeschooling Facebook groups, find your local homeschool moms and dig in. Those of us who have chosen it as well will always have your back. We get it, we understand. We know what it feels like to "be called" to homeschool.

When I decided to have children, I felt the great call to be a mother. I knew I wanted that more than anything else in the world, after wife. But then they started to grow, and I realized that I didn't want my motherhood call to end with kindergarten.

So I researched the best schools in the area. I visited those schools and was heartbroken by the dead eyes I saw in kindergarteners. Sure, they were learning French, but they didn't know how to play, dream, create! All things I wanted for my kids.

So I prayed. God loved my children and me. I knew this with all my heart. So I asked him what they needed. I went to him with my worries.

I said, "Lord, I do not want to bury my little lights under a bush by keeping them home. They need to bless others' lives."

He answered with "First, my daughter, they need to be lights that cannot be flushed out with the slightest wind, their time to shine will come. Build that light first that it might shine brighter"

Then I said, "but I want them tough, how will they be strong if they are home with me?"

His answer "I have plenty of tough children, what I need are children who are sensitive and sweet, who know my voice and know how to follow me. I will strengthen them my way"

I had my instructions. I never looked back. I have been called to educate my children. God has helped me and continues to help me. I am not alone. On the hard days I remember these words.

Mothers who educate their children at home have been called of God to educate the next generation His way. It is not a calling that we talk openly about in most circles. It is sacred. It is something we hold deep in our hearts. We can't always explain why we homeschool, we shouldn't have to defend our decision to anyone. It is our own personal calling and purpose in the world. We take it seriously, and know that we will be held accountable one day to God only. No matter what the state says.

He has guided us through every step. Math is as important to Him as history science and scripture. They are all his laws. He wants them taught truth. He wants our kids taught with love, curiosity, and creativity. These are his attributes, he wants us to be like Him.

Kiss My Curriculum

What I didn't expect, what has surprised me the most, was that I was being "homeschooled" as well. He didn't just use me to teach my kids, but he used my kids to teach me. We have been educated together. That is the most beautiful part. I never could have imagined the education I would receive at God's feet alongside my kids. Math, Science, History, all my least favorite subjects were retaught to me, I love them now. Writing? I flunked writing in high school, yet he has inspired me to write a book.

We have been personally called to teach our children. But that doesn't mean that the mother who doesn't homeschool her kids is any less. She also prays over her children, worries for them and does all she can. I have watched my sisters and sisters-in-law send their kids to school, then help to build the school and fight for the kids that they mother that aren't theirs. They fight administrations and teachers for morals to be taught and children to be protected. They volunteer in classes and put in endless hours to help. There is not one way to do things. We are each individually called to make a difference in our own spheres. It is not ours to judge, only to do what we can in our own circles. We are all trying to do the best we can and we should all have each other's back.

I personally was called to the homeschooling world. It is what I know, it is now my passion. Because of this "calling" to homeschool, we, all seven of us, are closer than we thought possible, reaching goals that were unattainable, and dreaming bigger than imaginable. Our minds have been opened to new possibilities. We needed homeschooling for us. Every family must choose for themselves.

For those who have chosen, like us, to homeschool, we are happy to share a few things we have learned along the way.

Kiss My Curriculum

Kiss My Curriculum

"It's not my credentials that qualify me to teach my child. IT IS MY GOD who made me qualified when he made me a MOM."

-Tamara L. Chilver

Lesson 2

Children Are Wonderful Presents

My children have taught me that they are not empty vessels to fill but wonderful presents with many layers to discover.

It's so funny how we are so excited to become parents and then as soon as these adorable little bundles come into the world we look around for everyone else to give us answers about how it should be done. It is the rare parent who can say, "I know what to do."

I started out as a mother who read about everything I could find about how to parent my kids.

Kiss My Curriculum

I would read parenting magazines, check out books from the library on their health, education, everything! I think everyone does this with the first baby. We want to get it right!

Then one day I was reading in *Parents Magazine* and felt this overwhelming sense of failure. These magazines were telling me everything I should be doing and everything I wasn't doing. I was so overrun by the idea that I would never be enough that I began to fall into a very deep depression. I realized that I could never be all the things that these books and magazines told me I needed to be. I began to question whether or not I even had it in me to be a good parent and started considering day care thinking that anyone but me would do a better job with my child. I turned to God with my worries, He has always helped me in my life. Why would this be any different? Then I heard the spirit say, "Stop reading what the so-called experts say and ask me! I am the expert on your child, I will help you!"

So I put the magazines and books away and used my scriptures instead. I decided to just enjoy my

Kiss My Curriculum

child and if I had questions (who doesn't), I would pray about it first, study my scriptures for the answer, and then let God tell me who to talk to. Many times the right friend would come along with the answers and insight I needed. Sometimes it was my mother or mother-in-law. Occasionally, it was my pediatrician or a professional.

I learned to check the sources these friends and professionals used before I took the advice. For example, did the friend that was giving me advice on behavior issues have kids with good behaviors? (Not often) Did the doctor that wrote the books about children actually have any? (You would be surprised how many "child Experts" don't have kids.) I was picky about whose advice I would take; My qualifications were not the same as the world's. I wanted exceptional kids, not just mediocre. I expected my children to change the world, not just get a well-paid job. I wanted them to help others, serve God, and make the world a better place for being in it. So I turned to the ultimate resource, God. He would be my ultimate and final source to guide me to where I needed to be. He had a whole new idea of what this all looked like. I had a lot to learn.

Heavenly Father also had a different idea about their school work. We started out homeschooling with workbooks and worksheets. We ended up frustrated, angry with each other, and feeling worthless. Those things didn't work for our children. (I wonder how much they work for any child.) So we learned to tailor learning to each child.

For example, our oldest was a natural learner. She taught herself to read and loved math and writing. She could sit for hours and teach herself. She would paint, draw, dance and sing for hours. She was so easy! I thought homeschooling was going to be a piece of cake. She now loves drama, dance, art, and spends her time in theater.

Our second child was also a natural learner but in a totally different way. She would not be coerced into anything at all, period. She didn't learn to read until she was around 8 years old. Because she didn't want to. Yes, I thought I was a failure, until I realized she just wasn't ready. However, that girl could fix anything in the house at a very young age. She fixed the washer, changed the battery in the car, repaired my broken jewelry, took apart and fixed broken mechanical toys. We called her "our tinker." She just loved to solve problems. To this day (she is 16) when I ask her what she would like to study she says, "I want to be a problem solver so I need to study everything I can." Now as she attends a charter part time they call on her to fix things all over the school, from theater to yearbook. Even the Vice Principal called her once to help fix her wedding dress.

Then #3 comes along and breaks all the rules in my head. Our first boy. He was born dead. They had to revive him. I knew then that this kid was going to try us.

As a baby, he was very easy. He was doted on by his 3-year-old and 2-year-old sisters. He went against all the "norms" that the doctors told us he should have. Everything was according to his timing. He didn't say his first word ("Mama") until he was three. (We wondered if he would ever speak at all.) Then over night, he wouldn't stop talking. He didn't read until he was 10. There was nothing I could do to convince him. Once he decided to read, he learned in a few weeks. He took everything apart and tried to figure everything out. As long as I didn't put a pencil in his hand he was happy.

When he was about 4 years old we were driving down the highway and my son was unusually quiet. Then out of nowhere he declared very excitedly that he has figured it out. He gets how the cars move and steer. Then he proceeded to explain to me how a car axle works. He had been observing the cars from the back seat of the minivan the whole time and had decided to figure out how they work. He was dang accurate. That is when I realized that a child will learn what they want when they want. I also learned that observation is a powerful teacher.

I have two children who learned to read around the age of 5. The other three had no interest until they were 7-10 years old. It used to bother me that they weren't all early readers. According to the experts the earlier they read the better, right?

Kiss My Curriculum

As a mother, I was deeply worried that I had failed my children. I thought, "Maybe I should push them more?" I tried that with my second child until I realized she just didn't care. But then again why should she? I started wondering what was wrong with having a child being read to for as long as possible? These children would nuzzle against me or my husband for reading time; they loved it as much as we did. Over the years we have read thousands of books together. It is still such a comfort to them that even as 16 and 17-year-olds, they get out their art and sit nearby whenever dad pulls out a book to read aloud. It doesn't matter that they had read the book before. They usually don't even care what book it is. They just love to cuddle up and let him read.

I now realize that maybe late reading was my children's way of saying, "I would rather cuddle you and hear your voice than be alone." I am grateful that I made a habit of reading aloud and let them read independently at a later time. They all have a love for reading now.

Kiss My Curriculum

Our favorite days of the week are library days. We spend an hour at the library and load up on books, then come home, pop popcorn, and read the entire afternoon. I read aloud to them until I inevitably fall asleep, then they will read for themselves or look at pictures.

My favorite moments were when my older kids would cuddle with the younger ones and read to them. Those moments are magical. I learned that the younger kids could learn just as well from the older ones, and that the older kids were learning how to teach. Win-win for all. The children learned a lot from those books, but they learned more from all that cuddle time with each other. They learned we are a team in our education. That they are loved by each other as much as their parents. These experiences slowly taught me that there were better ways for my children to be educated than simply following a workbook. Maybe this could be a better way for other children too.

Kiss My Curriculum

What about Math?

First, homeschoolers will never be at the "levels" that public schooled kids are at. Why? because we do it differently.

For example math. All of my kids pick up math quickly at young ages. Because they notice at a very young age when someone gets more cookies then they do. Counting comes with making sure life is even. "She has more candy than me" gets them understanding adding and subtracting very quickly.

But my kids are always "behind" their peers in math for one reason. I don't give Bs or Cs! My kids don't move on in math with a B or a C. They understand it and move on, or they don't understand it enough and we need more time on the subject.

I will not let them "slip by" with a limited understanding in math. So it takes longer, sometimes. Sometimes they get it quickly and we move on. But I don't care what the schools say about where they "should be" because my kids study percentages and decimals until they can do it in their heads.

Kiss My Curriculum

They must be able to handle money, interest, and cash flow. Those are percentages. My kids may never study calculus, but they will never be taken advantage of because of the lack of knowledge over interest or percentages. So we spend years on those because they will be used the most.

So do I care if they are "at grade level" in Math? NO WAY! I want them better educated than that!

What about the arts?

As a homeschool mom, I always felt that art, music, and anything creative was vital to educating my children. We danced almost every day. Not because it was on the schedule but because it was natural to turn on the music at the end of the day as we cleaned the house. We always sang at the top of our lungs and danced together as we cleaned. I started doing it as a young mom of toddlers just for fun. But once you start something good, you can't help but keep doing it. Days turned into years, and now my teens will turn on the music when it is cleaning time and sing and dance with me with complete abandon. We even sing

Kiss My Curriculum

at the tops of our lungs in the car: Hamilton, The Greatest Showman, whatever is their current favorites. We have exposed them to a lot of musicals this way and have grown closer as a family too.

Music has played a central role in our homeschool, especially during our creative times. We always played music during art time. This was generally classical. Something soothing was our favorite during cold or rainy days. I would turn on soothing music and we would come up with an art project. What started out as play dough when they were younger has turned into beautiful oil paintings, 3D paper dragons the size of an adult, origami everything. You name it the kids have done it and loved it. Their art skills have all expanded to their favorite mediums and they are becoming masters.

There was a time where our lives became intensely overscheduled and I noticed that my 3 older teens were struggling with depression. I prayed hard to know how to help them; I didn't want my kids to struggle like so many teens do. The answer I received floored me once again: "What are they creating?" It's when I get these random but clearly inspired answers that I know that the answers aren't just in my head but are direct revelation. They usually surprise me.

In response to this answer, I sat down with each of my older children and asked them if they were creating anything. Each said it had been a while. So we sat down to plan a project for each of them, created a shopping list, and got to work. One child needed more gems for her jewelry making. One needed new brushes for her paints. One just needed me to sit with him as he looked on YouTube for ideas.

Once they were set up for their projects, they disappeared into their rooms. I really missed them! But I would check on them occasionally to see if they needed anything. When I would ask, "Whatcha doing?" all of their answers were, "Creating!" After only a few days, there was a bounce in their step. All three of them were happier, and they were excited to finish up their other responsibilities so that they could get back to their projects. It was an easy solution to what can be a big problem. There were no doctors, no therapists, no diet changes – just a place to focus their creativity. It was miraculous.

Creating is a God-like attribute. It is through his joy in creation that we were made. I find that I, too, am happiest when I have some sort of creative project in the wings (Sometimes I have several). It is when I don't have one to think about during downtime that I get anxiety and depression. My children have now discovered the same for themselves and have learned that creative projects need to be a major priority in their curriculum. My teens now go to a charter school, but have determined to go only part-time so that they still have time to work on their own Ideas. This was their choice, not mine.

Will They Be Ready?

Our "life schooling" way of educating our kids has made me question if they will be ready for the "real world". Or at least it did, until I realized that this way of educating shapes minds and hearts in a different and possibly more profound way than other, more traditional methods of teaching.

An example of this happened when my oldest decided to try a science class at the high school her 8th grade year. We have always loved science in our family. It has been more of a constant discussion than memorized facts. My husband is a NASA engineer after all, so it was just a part of our lives. Our daughter was a little nervous that she wouldn't be able to keep up with the other kids in the class, but decided to move forward and find out for certain anyway.

Just a week or so into the class she came home ecstatic about an experience she had that day. The teacher had given a problem and they were to come up with a scientific solution as a group. She was the youngest in her group (the rest were juniors and seniors), and the problem required math she had never done. She said that even though the other kids knew some of the math, they couldn't understand how to fix the problem using that math. So she took it on as a challenge and was the only one in the class to solve the problem correctly, even though she didn't have the math knowledge.

We both learned that day that her creativity and problem solving skills were what allowed her to see solutions where others could not and ultimately lead to her victory that day. She learned that she valued these vital skills, and was grateful for a homeschool where her mother let her solve her own problems. (I was probably just too tired to help the poor girl.)

Now that our kids are in the charter school system, they are discovering just how rare they are. They're seeing how differently they think and act from other students, but they see it as strengths, because they are. They love to take on challenges, lead groups, start projects, and dive into things that other kids are not willing to do. They often get frustrated at the laziness around them, but they are discovering that they have a lot to offer the world. So will they be ready and prepared to go to college, have a job, be adults? I am now more sure of it than ever.

Kiss My Curriculum

They know how to think, how to analyze, and how to negotiate. They will be just fine.

Kiss My Curriculum

"A person who never made a mistake never tried anything new."

-Albert Einstein

Lesson 3

There Is No Failure, Only Try

Anyone who has ever seen a toddler has heard the emphatic phrases, "I DO IT!" or "Let me do it!" We all know that small children have no fear of falling, some of them to the detriment of their own safety.

I have always wanted to protect my children, just like any good parent does. I love their independence and reveled in it! Until there is a threat of failure or disappointment. Then I wanted to protect them from all pain. But Children are born to success. God created them to succeed. He created all of us to succeed. But we have to fail occasionally to understand what that even means, so that we know what we are working for. My children quickly taught me that they had a right to feel failure and the pain that often accompanies it. They wanted to taste it as much as success.

Every parent wants what is best for their children. Every parent would like to spare their kids the pain of the failures we have faced in life. It is good that we feel this way, it is part of being protective. It allows us to help them to move above and beyond where we have been. But I learned that too much protection can hinder and block our children's growth as well. My husband's mother was raised by a mother who was so worried that her children would get hurt that they were never allowed to ride a bike, roller-skate, play a sport, or swim. I have watched as my husband's aunts and uncles have lived with that fear set in their lives into their 60s. I think it is tragic.

My husband and I are not as protective, but we each have different levels of protection depending on the activity.

Kiss My Curriculum

I saw myself protecting them in small ways when they were younger, I loved doing art projects with my kids and would show them how to create something. They would start doing it "wrong" (in my opinion), so I would "fix" it for them. When they stopped doing art projects with me, I couldn't figure out why. Eventually, one of my daughters said, "Because you won't let me do it."

I was afraid they would do the project wrong and not like their work. So I was helping them make it "look pretty" or "right". That made them lose interest in the project altogether. Essentially, what I thought was imperfect work from them, I perceived as a failure, and I didn't want them to fail. But they never saw their creations as failure. The only failure was mine when I didn't them do it their own way.

My kids have taught me that only through failure can we discover who we are and what talents we have. Some things work out and show us great things about ourselves. Some things don't work out, but they teach us great attributes and qualities about ourselves. It is a child's right and privilege to fail beautifully so that they might discover who they are and what they have to offer this world. If they were never allowed to fail they would also never have the opportunity to succeed. I have learned to love to watch them do both.

Allowing children to fail, means allowing them to try. You can't have one without the other. I didn't learn that lesson in one afternoon. I was extremely slow in learning it – years in fact. I have been better at letting them try, but it is often extremely painful and nail-biting for me.

Our kids have always been careful naturally; we are no daredevils for sure. Each child is a little more daring than the last, but I wonder if that is because we are learning to relax more with each child.

I have always pushed my kids to ride bikes, rollerblade, climb hills and roll down them etc. My husband cringes when this happens but stands by with the first aid kit (we are all klutzes). On the flipside, when it came time to try out for a play, a singing gig, or sort of emotional or mental challenge, my husband was 100% behind those risks. This is where I struggled. I knew how to fix a scraped knee or broken bone, But not a broken heart. A broken heart felt like a bigger risk for me.

When our neighbors came to us to see if our 5-year-old wanted to try out for a local theater production, I was against it. I didn't want her to not get the part and be heartbroken. My husband convinced me that it would be ok and to let her try. She got the part, and her love of musical theater was born at five. She has since landed every part she has tried out for; theater is her passion. Where would she be if I had "protected" her and held her back from her first opportunity in the theater?

Yes, all of her success in the theater sounds lovely, of course, until you place her little sister, only 12 months younger, into the picture. After watching her sister be in theater, she wanted to be in the theater too. She has been in every play her sister has been in, but rarely the part she wants. She has been the supporting role to her sister her entire life. It has been extremely hard for her. In her eyes, she has failed many times.

Kiss My Curriculum

Her failures haven't stopped her, though. Instead of getting discouraged over lost roles, she has decided to try out other things in theater that her sister didn't want to do. She now designs costumes, works the mics, lights, and staging. The directors have come to rely on her to make sure the show is working. They turn to her to fix issues, mend costumes, and solve other behind-the-scenes problems. Her perceived failure at not getting lead parts has helped her discover her strengths in the other areas of theater. I wanted to protect her from trying out at all. She has shed a few disappointed tears. But through it all she has discovered talents and interests she didn't know she had.

Our children love trying new things, and as they do, I am always worried about the failure that may come. I will often ask them, "If you go for this, how will you feel if you get it? How will you feel if you don't?" Their answers to the latter always amaze me. It is always with confidence that they say things like, "Then I don't," or "Then I will get involved anyway."

Kiss My Curriculum

Our two oldest daughters ran for student office one year. One as a junior and one as a sophomore. The older daughter won. The younger did not. This was after a dance tryout and a play tryout where the older daughter got everything she wanted and the younger one didn't get anything she wanted. We were thrilled for the older one of course. But equally devastated for the younger one.

I went to her room one evening to see how she was taking it. I was afraid to find her in tears. Instead, I found her on her bed with her scriptures and journal open. She seemed at peace. I sat on her bed and asked her how she was doing with all of this. She said proudly, "I am so happy for Alexa; she deserves it. I am sad for me, but I guess the Lord wants something else for me. I will stay involved and be a part of it all. I guess I just have a different path." She continues to help in all the areas she "failed" in, but she tells me she is learning what is not for her. By doing so she is discovering what IS for her.

Our older children have mirrored my husband and I in our beliefs about risk. But our younger two children seem to defy who we were and instead reflect the people we have come to be. These two don't even know the meaning of the word failure. Not because they haven't fallen down, but because they see falling as just part of life. Falling and getting back up is what they do.

Our youngest, Benny has especially taught us all what it means to fall. He is famous for falling hard, and with blood dripping down his knees, jumping up to say, "I'm ok!" You almost miss the tears falling down his face through his enthusiasm. When he was three, we were in Hawaii on a family vacation. He was playing at the water's edge, within a few feet of me, when a huge wave hit him from behind, dragged him down, and completely covered him. I panicked and went running, but before I could reach him he jumped back up and yelled at the top of his lungs, **"THAT WAS AWESOME! CAN I DO IT AGAIN?"**

He teaches us every day that falling down can be awesome. Failure and falling bring an adventure of their own. If you keep this perspective, then there is no failure, just a new adventure. Thanks to Benny I am seeing my failures more like this all the time. As I have had some pretty big failures in my life, my children have put their arms around me and said, "It's ok, Mom; we'll just get back up again!"

Fighting Children

This leads into another daily issue in every parent's life. Children fighting. If your children are fighting, it is not a failure of either the parent or the child. It is just part of the "learning" that goes on in a safe place, your home.

How do you get children to get along? This is a huge parenting question that I hear all the time. Everyone has their methods, several of which I've tried: time outs, point charts, revoked privileges, withheld allowance , you name it. None of them seemed to stick for us and that was discouraging.

One day I was on the phone talking to my sister about how I was going crazy with all the fighting. Let's face it, seven people all in the house together day-in and day-out with few other social interactions can make you a little crazy. She asked me what I was doing to combat the fighting. After I gave her a list of all the things I had tried without success, she gave me one piece of advice that changed our parenting forever. She said, "The punishment in the house should not give you more work; it should *relieve* you of work. That way, when they fight, you get rewarded!"

To be honest I didn't get it at first. She had to spell it out for me, which was easy since it only takes four words. "You fight, you clean." That is all I have to say to get the fighting to stop. Sure, it took some training, but before I knew it, fights were few and far between.

Here is what it looks like:

I am working in another room and hear a fight beginning. I say, "You fight, you clean." Some days that is all it takes, and they work out their differences peacefully and get back to playing.

Kiss My Curriculum

Normally, though, that's only the first warning. The second time I hear the fighting I walk in and without asking whose fault it was or what happened, I say, "You're fighting. Isaac, bathroom; Nicole, kitchen floor; Ben, garbage. You have 10 minutes, go! Anyone not done in 10 minutes gets another job". They jump and run, always with complaining. But I respond with, "If you complain, you get more jobs!" They try to point fingers at the guilty one. I generally tell them, "You could have walked away. You're down to 9 minutes..."

It sounds mean, but let me explain the beauty of this. So much good comes from these four small words. First, this removes myself as judge and jury. I don't have to decide who is wrong and who was right, which means no one's feelings are hurt by me or walks away thinking I have been unfair, and they learn that I will not pick sides.

Second, they learn that if they had walked away from the argument before warning 2 came they would not be cleaning. Walking away is easier by far. Third, they learn how to clean. Over the years they have become good, fast cleaners! Fourth, I get a break. They are removed from each other and are no longer fighting, plus, they're doing chores that I then won't have to do myself. They learn that if what they are doing makes my life harder, then they will also be the one to make my life easier.

Finally, over the years they have learned how to work out their differences without a mediator. I have heard them many times start an argument only for one of them to quickly remind the others that if mom hears them fighting they will all have to clean. So they apologize to each other so they can continue playing. There has been one day in 50 that they will play all day like this, and it is wonderful!

Generally, though, the chores inevitably happen because a fight ensues. I let them play until the fight comes, then they work on homework and jobs. Their fighting lets me know when a change is needed. A few hours of cleaning and homework puts them back into playing well together.

My oldest kids have learned other lessons over the years. For example, they recognize when the "play magic" has ended and the fights are coming, so they leave the situation before it gets ugly and mom gets involved. They are aware of feelings in a room and know how to deal with escalating situations. Sometimes they want the magic to continue, so they pacify the offended ones. Other times they know when the situation can no longer be saved and they simply walk away. I have seen them do the same in other social situations with their cousins and friends. They are peacemakers who know how to put out fires and redirect the group. All because of "You fight, you clean."

I didn't know what good would come from this habit when we started. I couldn't know what the results would be. It was a risk. But I chose to do the thing that allowed ME the most peace. Now it has become a joke in the house. I will often tease them in the morning, "Hey guys, I could really use some fighting today; I have a lot that needs to get done." This will often spark some extra careful behavior, and I will get a lot more done. The key to any punishment, reward system, or philosophy in the house, is that it rewards mom the most. Oh and keeping it simple; if it is hard to maintain, it won't last and you'll have to find something that will. Or just use our idea. You fight, you clean. Period.

Kiss My Curriculum

"A Teaching degree is to homeschooling as a culinary degree is to Grandma's cooking. It just can't touch the love, care and personal standard that only she can stir in."

-Dawn Shelton

Lesson 4

Rhythms, Routines, and Atmosphere

Don't apologize for the mess

I have never had a Pinterest style home. I always wanted one, but I just don't have the knack. But one thing I have always been very aware of is how my home FELT. I always wanted people to walk into my home and feel like they belonged. Like they could step through the doors, take off the world, and just be them. I don't believe having a picture-worthy home does that.

Early in motherhood, I had two girls under the age of three. I remember I couldn't keep the house clean. It didn't matter what I did, those two would pull

43

everything out. So I started to come to terms with not cleaning until they went to sleep. "Why waste my energy?" was my thought.

One day a woman from my church stopped in to see me. When she walked through the door she had to step over a ton of toys. The dishes were piled in the sink, and I was a mess. My first inclination was to apologize for the mess, but my bad-attitude-self decided I had nothing to apologize for: I had two babies, I was tired, my husband was a full time student, and worked full-time. This woman just surprised me with a visit; if she didn't like my house, I really didn't care.

She talked to me for a second, then surprised me by saying something I have remembered ever since. "Thank you for not apologizing for the mess. I know I surprised you. I know you are tired and busy. I love that you are who you are without apologies. It's one of my favorite things about you. It's why your children are so happy. Your house is exactly how it should be at this time in your life. Keep up the good work." Then she left.

Kiss My Curriculum

I stood there shocked; I am sure my mouth was hanging open. She taught me a very powerful lesson. Don't apologize for the mess. Not the mess in my house, not the mess in my head. It is all a part of who I am, where I am now and where I am going. I learned to love that toy mess. It meant that I had active children at my house. One day my house will be clean, but there will be no child living there. I don't look forward to the days when I won't have the ones who make the mess.

My favorite quote is from "Yours, Mine and Ours." This is one of our favorite movies because I am just like the mother and my husband is like the father. In the midst of utter disaster, Helen North is asked if she would host something at her home where she lives with her 10 children. She answers, "Oh no! Homes are for self-expression, NOT good impressions!"

The first time I saw that movie, I had no kids. I had a quiet house, and all I could think was, "Now that's what I want! I want a crazy house with creative kids running everywhere!" Beautiful! I now have that house, and I love it!

Some days I do hate it and want to run and hide. When it is time to clean it, I want to cry. Luckily I don't believe that it is solely my job to clean the house. If the kid can walk, the kid can clean. That's our philosophy. All our children do jobs daily to keep the house clean. Our rule, "You fight, you clean" keeps the house orderly as well. But you already know that.

I have been told often that people like the feel of our home. I have spent time analyzing why and how we have a certain feeling in our home. It is what I have always wanted, but I am not sure what I have done. Even in the midst of mess, I have had people tell me that we have a safe, spiritual feeling in our home.

The more I've pondered, the more I think I understand what we've done to help create such an atmosphere. 1. God is always first 2. Spouse is always second 3. Kids are always third.

Put God First

We put God first by reading scriptures and praying often. No, we are not 100% consistent; we aren't robots. We do our best with the scriptures. Once they can read on their own, it is their required daily reading. We attend church, we serve others. When my husband or I have church responsibilities, we take as many kids as we can under appropriate circumstances. We try to make the house a place that God can reside. Nothing is allowed in that could offend him. We are also careful to only allow people in our home that would not offend the spirit we have. That may seem extreme to some, but our home is our safe haven. Not even family members that carry a bad spirit are invited. We can meet them somewhere else. We also have a media rule. If the person on the TV or Movie are not the kind of people we would allow into our home, then they can't come in, including through media.

Spouse is always second

My husband and I both put God first. Which means putting each other second is really first as well. I go to my Father in Heaven with my complaints against my husband. Not to my friends or siblings. God corrects the one that needs the correction. Sometimes its him and sometimes it's me. But it's always miraculous what he does.

Date night should be as sacred as church on Sunday. This wasn't always easy when they were young. We lived out of state away from family, so date night was a movie night. But now that they are older and don't need a sitter they have come to count on that night and help us get out of the house. If we kiss or hold hands they love to act like they are grossed out. But when they do, they always have a smile on their faces. They know that if Mom and Dad are ok then life will be fine.

It wasn't always romantic. Sometimes kids just get in the way. It happens. Romance is like a constant fight that feels like you are always losing. We keep fighting and so far we are winning.

Kids are third

Our kids know that we adore them. They know that we have and will give up everything in this world for them. But we will not offend God for them, and we will not let them get in the way of our marriage. When they are little that was not clear. Crying babies have to come first. They just do. As they have gotten older we have had to set the limits more clearly for them. One of our rules is that we get to sit by each other in church. They will try to get in-between us, but it is a boundary we have clearly set. Like many others. I have found that once the boundaries are set they are happier knowing their place. They love to see us put each other first.

Bedtime is a great place to teach the order of our priorities, and it is an easy place where we can put God first. We read to the kids, have them brush their teeth, and put on PJs. Then we pray with them, as a family, and individually in their rooms then sing them a primary song. This is when we like to discuss how their day was. Sometimes we do this while lying down with them and cuddling, sometimes a quick kiss on the cheek. Bedtime for us has taken 1 hour minimum because of the one-on-one time we try to give each child.

We have always put them to bed early, telling them that it is Mommy and Daddy time. We rarely had to explain that it was important that we had this time together so that we could stay in love. It has been worth it. Even when my husband was busy with school or other responsibilities, he would come home at night in time for bed and do bedtime with each child. Often he would leave for his other responsibilities right after bed, but he didn't let anything get in the way of that time if he could help it. Some years it was the only time he saw them all day, and it was a sacred time for them and him.

I am eternally grateful for him doing that. I had spent all day with them, I didn't like bedtime. All I wanted to do was get them to bed so I could take a break. It was the perfect partnership. Thanks to him they did get their spiritual time almost every night as he leads them in prayer. How great is a righteous Father? How blessed is the child who has a Daddy that adores them? A Knight in shining armor doesn't show up on a white horse in my house (he is allergic); he shows up in a working man's clothes with soft hands, a loving heart, and pure joy in his children and teaching them to love God.

Atmosphere. Display their work

One thing that was important to us was to show the kids how much we loved the work they created. We designated a wall in our house for their artwork, and they loved filling it. In one house the wall was in our bedroom; in another, it was the wall that ran along the staircase. It changed from house to house, but we loved having the kids decorate and display their work.

As they got older, the art got better and better. It slowly became framed and center of a room. We currently have a wall as you walk in the house with their canvases all over it. We get a lot of comments about the art and people are impressed that we would show their art in such a prominent place. I think having their art on display makes it feel more like home. Plus it instills confidence in our kids and tells them that their art is precious to us and good enough for us to show off.

Change things up

Our home is also full of the things our kids love to do. Though we try to make each room beautiful, each room is for use, not show. We have a front room with drums, guitars, violins, and a piano. All instruments that are out get used. Once it's put in a case, we find that they are no longer played. So we keep instruments on the wall or on stands in a classy way, so that our children will be drawn in to play them. It works.

Once we moved the piano to a place that made it prettier for the house but out of the way of the natural flow of the kids. They stopped playing it. When we moved it to a more central location, they played it more. I find that moving around rooms in the house and changing things up makes old toys and art supplies interesting again. So we reorganize often. When even something gets old and boring or art or music in the house slow down, I rearrange furniture and rooms to make it more appealing. It works every time.

We have tried to have a "homeschool room" but found that our education wasn't something that belonged in one room of the house. In order to instill the love of education in our kids, they needed to be able to read in a tree, in a hammock, or on a couch. Our best learning is always done at the dinner table or couch. My well organized "homeschool rooms" often became just a storage space for the educational curriculum we didn't really need.

Everything always ended up on the dinner table. No matter what I tried the projects were right there in the kitchen. Some fights I just have to give up. Thankfully, being flexible is my greatest skill, so we often eat at the kitchen counter because we are in the middle of a project that requires the dinner table and can't be cleaned up yet.

Kiss My Curriculum

Like a homeschool room, a toy room is also just a waste of space. Kids want to be near their parents, not shut away from them. They would move from room to room as I would, so I made sure to have a learning and play object for them everywhere. That way we could take advantage of a moment. I could clean a room, do laundry, or clean a bathroom and they could play or do learning activities with me as I went about my duties. The important thing for us has been to make every room in the house a room of learning. We have instruments in one room, art in another, and toys and building materials mixed in between. It results in a better flow.

Throw out the schedule

People often ask me how I got my kids on a good homeschool schedule. Since I homeschool, people think we must be really organized. The answer to their question? I don't! We as humans do not operate naturally on a schedule! So how do I "get" my kids to get anything done? It's called Rhythm. Our bodies have natural rhythms and so do our homes and lives. Once you recognize those rhythms and work with them instead of against them, you can actually learn more and stress less.

Yearly Rhythm

The best way to understand this is to go broad, so we'll begin with the yearly rhythm. This rhythm is seasonal and God-made. The months, remember, are man-made schedules. The seasons were created by someone far grander, so if we look at the seasons for what to learn and how to act, we will find a very natural way of living and learning.

For example, in the winter, my kids love to cuddle up and read books. Why? Because it's cold outside and they want to be indoors. This is the time we pop a lot of popcorn, and read books alone or as a family. It's also a time for art. We play soft music and do art for weeks on end in those cold months.

We generally have a family book going during the winter months that we read together once or twice a week. (Dad reads; We do art). We try to make our family read-aloud one of the classics or a book about one of the greats in history. We read about Benjamin Franklin, Thomas Jefferson, Eleanor Roosevelt, and more. My kids learn a lot of science and history this way and don't even know it. We get through a lot of books in the winter. We also go through a lot of art supplies and "reading snacks".

Then spring comes. We are all itching to get outside, especially in the evenings. Family reading comes to a pause once the evenings are nice. Why read to a kid who is staring out the window wishing they could be outside? So take them outside and teach them there! Kids are fascinated by all the baby animals and changes that happen in the spring, so this became a great time for microscopes, exploring, and asking questions. We spend a lot of time looking at bugs, planting flowers and vegetables, and learning about herbs. As it warms up we take every advantage of learning outside, including the best science lesson ever: camping. Our natural rhythms crave these things in their season, so we do them.

Kiss My Curriculum

By the heat of summer the kids are ready to be inside during the heat of the day. They want to play with their public schooled friends and I use that as a motivator to get some work done. I've found this is a great time to get math, writing, "clerical work" done as their motivation is playing with friends. This is when my kids handwritten work does the best. Though we do some during the other months as well, this is when they really excel.

Then Fall comes, something about the changes in the seasons, always makes us want more art. But as it gets colder and we move into winter we crave books and cuddling again.

When I plan our learning according to the natural rhythms of the seasons, their questions support that time and the learning doesn't even feel like its forced. It's just life.

Kiss My Curriculum

Weekly Rhythms (Routines?)

We have weekly rhythms as well. Monday and Tuesday our minds are fresh from the rest we received Sunday, so we are generally ready for a challenge or something new. These are great days for learning new concepts. By Wednesday we are tired from the intense first two days. So we call it library day and spend the morning in the library piling on books. We head home to a read-a-thon. Everyone by themselves with their own books. In winter they are curled up in front of the fireplace. In summer they are in a tree, hammock, or out on a blanket on the grass.

Thursdays we are all ready to get some space from each other. This is perfect for play dates, co-ops, and activities with others. Friday we work on a house project in the morning or catch up on chores, but mostly we play. My kids get video games, movies, hiking, pool time, you name it. After lunch on Friday's they get to do what they want if all their homework for the week is done. They have come to cherish this time of freedom.

Kiss My Curriculum

Saturday is "Daddy Day." Mom gets to take it off, if she needs to. Dad leads a family project or just plays with the kids. My kids count down the days until "Daddy Day." Following these weekly rhythms allows the kids time to rest bodies and brains as needed. But they also get to learn what they crave, when they crave it.

Daily Rhythm

Our daily rhythm looks like this: Wake up slowly and play together quietly (my kids always play the best in the morning hours together). I might sleep in if I have had a rough night with a baby, or I might be working out if I had a good night. We eat breakfast, once we are hungry. After breakfast, we work on math and writing. After lunch, we have quiet time or project time. Once projects are done, we have play time until it's time to clean the house and make dinner. Then we have dinner, family time, and head to bed.

Notice not once did I show a time we do these things. We don't live by the clock. It is not our master; we are its master! Yes, we have doctor's appointments and other things that require exact times. We schedule those during our most natural routines. We never schedule them in the mornings; those are sacred to us, but we find that right after lunch feels more natural for these appointments. They match our rhythm.

I have tried job charts, schedules, and stopwatches. What I found was stress and feeling like we worked for someone. I always felt that I should be checking in with a boss to let him know I had obtained the desired results that day (maybe even with a salute). But year after year I started hiding the clocks. I began to do what felt right in a given moment, instead of what I had been told should be doing. It was only as I got rid of the clocks, I started to see the patterns in our lives. I allowed those patterns to create routines and our family's natural rhythms created a happier family.

Each family has their own rhythms. Some families are night owls; some are early risers. Your rhythms will change as your kids grow. If you have babies, your rhythms are different than if you don't have babies. The key is to be open to constant change and trust that the rhythms will take care of the rest.

Pay attention to the natural rhythms in your family and your stress will melt away the more your rigid schedules do. Trust the seasons. Lap up those lazy season (yes, there's one of those) and work hard in the other seasons So, new homeschool moms, throw away your checklists. Play, cuddle, read. Trust that God already has done the planning for you, and follow your heart to create the rhythm, routines, and atmosphere that will best serve your unique family.

"It is not that I'm worried if my kids go to school they won't turn out "OK". Homeschool is about so much more. The Family time is a treasure. The relationships, the learning, the lifestyle, the discipleship. It's not about keeping them from something-It doesn't shelter- IT FREES!"

-Karen DeBeus

Lesson 5

Socialization? They turned out just like me!!!

Yes, we homeschooled. At the time we started we felt homeschooling was superior to all other forms of education. Why? Because we were doing it and we needed to feel that it was the right thing no matter what.

After 20 years of homeschooling, charter schooling, private schooling, and everything in between we have a new opinion. First, every kid needs their own thing. From child to child we had to change up curriculum, classes, and needs. Second, every family has its own needs. What we did for our

Kiss My Curriculum

kids' many people don't do for their kids, but they still raise great kids! Third, regardless of how a family chose to educate their family (we met a lot of homeschooled families, public schooled families, and private schooled families), the bottom line was that each one of those kids turned into one form or another of their parents. No matter what you try to teach your children, or how that is taught, your kids will turn out to be you.

For example, while my kids were young I spent a lot of time and effort putting together co-ops with other kids around us so that they could learn things I couldn't or didn't want to teach them. One of those endeavors included organizing over 50 kids into a gymnastics homeschool class so that we could get discounted rates and classes during the day. I also organized my friends into groups so that each Thursday they would come to my house and each mother would take a topic. We did science, history, art, and theater. I put all of these things together so that my kids would learn these topics and skills.

Kiss My Curriculum

The Interesting thing is that they don't remember much of those classes. Instead, they all organize groups to do the fun activities they want to do. They have started game night in the neighborhood, organize service projects, and are now in student body organizing dances and fundraisers. I thought I was teaching them academic subjects; instead, they turned out just like me organizing events and activities as they feel a need or a want.

You really can't choose what your kids learn from you, for better or worse. Most of our kids have my attitude, our love of hard work, and our love of service. All of which stemmed from them helping me plan funerals, feed sick neighbors, and do yard work for others. They always had to come along when I did these things. So while, they don't remember a lot of the science projects we did, they do remember how to organize one and serve others.

I believe the best thing that we did was accidentally teach them to be their best selves. We have always tried to strive to be better people. So that is what they do now. There are some things they have picked up from us that we don't always like: my need for an occasional cuss word is one of them and the fact that I struggle with authority figures (go figure). They leave their shoes in the middle of the room on the floor. One of my kids do that all the time, and it drives me crazy! It drives my husband even crazier when I do it, too.

We have weird friends that homeschool their kids. We also have weird friends that public schooled their kids. Both families have weird kids. We have "cool" friends in both groups as well. And their kids are cool, too. We fool ourselves into thinking we teach our children anything. They simply observe us and decide what to keep and what to throw way. We don't get to control what they take from us . The best we can do is control what they observe from us. If we are being our best selves, our kids will become greater. I think our kids surpassed us at the age of 2. But remember, if we are lazy, mean, or grumpy, they will outdo us there, too.

My children taught me that they would turn into the person I actually was much faster than the person I was trying to get them to become. I learned the principle "Do as I say, not as I do" is a farce. I learned this the hard way, of course. Over the years this lesson was repeated to me through different experiences.

The very first time this hit home was when our third child, a boy, was about 1 year old. We had moved to a new house and I had a big heavy wall mirror that I had set on the floor and laid against the wall in a dining room where we had no furniture. Our two daughters, 4 and 5 years old, very quickly learned how fun this mirror could be and would be put on their princess dresses and dance in front of it for hours acting out their favorite Disney movies. I was amazed at how long it would entertain them, so I let them spend as much time there as they wanted. I could get so much done; it was a miracle!

Remember, I grew up with very low self-esteem. I was determined that my children grow up differently. I always talked to my daughters about how wonderful they were. I didn't want them to think they were fat, ugly, or incompetent, but to be honest, those were things I thought about and told myself. So I fought those ideas on their behalf with words of encouragement.

I was a bit worried about turning my daughters into self-centered divas, especially with the mirror always where they could admire themselves. A family friend told my parents once that she believed her job as a mother was to build up her children as best she could; she would let God do the humbling. I loved that, so it became my philosophy – build them up all we could and let God humble them as necessary; he is kinder than I am.

So with this idea, I let my kids dance in front of that mirror as much as they could stand. Except, not my son. We moved again and for a little bit of time, I put the mirror on the floor. My son was learning to crawl but hadn't seen his reflection as much as his sisters had. I am not even sure he had seen it at all the first year of his life. One day I picked him up to look at himself in the mirror, and like all mothers do, I introduced my son to himself in the mirror. It was always one of my favorite things because my daughters loved what they saw.

I had no idea how different my experience with my son would be. I held him up to the mirror and he refused to look. I was surprised. When I finally got him to look at himself, he flinched and looked away, as if he saw something he didn't like . He was one year old! I had never seen that before, except in my nephew who had been adopted after severe abuse.

My heart broke. We were a loving family who adored this boy; how could he hate his reflection? So I put the big mirror on the floor again, with the hope that he would spend some time in front of it. All he did was avoid it.

This really bothered me, so I prayed about what to do. The thought came, "What do you do when you see YOUR reflection?" Wait, what?! I had never thought of that. I had been struggling with my self-esteem a lot during that period. I was carrying an extra 40 pounds I couldn't get it off and I was tired and really struggling emotionally.

Kiss My Curriculum

I realized that I didn't like my reflection at all, but I didn't realize I was avoiding the mirror or flinching at my reflection. I hadn't even considered that my son a 1-year-old would be the one to copy his mother's reaction to the mirror. The girls were doing what I said; he was doing what I did.

The idea that he would be my worst me was painful and scary. My poor baby deserved a better mother, but I didn't know where to start. At first, I thought that I needed to be thin to be able to like myself in the mirror. But I didn't want my son to wait that long.

So I started a game. I would put my son in my lap, and we would sit on the floor in front of the mirror. At first, I tried to talk about all the wonderful things I saw in him, but he wouldn't have it and would crawl away. So I tweaked my plan. I sat in front of the mirror by myself and commented out loud on my strengths: physical, mental, and spiritual. I know that this seems a little creepy, like the witch in Snow White, but I figured if he was going to copy me I had better do what I wanted him to do.

Kiss My Curriculum

So I started out by just looking and smiling at myself. I tried to sit in front of the mirror more, dance with my kids in the mirror more, and I started to "perform" with them in front of the mirror. Slowly, my son joined us.

I would love to be able to tell you that it fixed him and his self-esteem was perfect after that. But it wasn't that easy. He is my kid who has always struggled a bit with his reflection. Even as he got older 10-12 years old he would say, "Mom, I just don't like my reflection." Thankfully, he didn't hide from the mirror anymore, and around the age of 12-13, he started liking what he saw.

Coincidentally, this was actually a time of great confidence for me as well. I also liked what I saw in the mirror. It took both of us over 10 years of talking positively to ourselves in the mirror, even when we didn't feel it, to finally believe the words we were saying. It wasn't until I stopped thinking, "My hair is too thin," "My cheeks are too big," " I wish I were thinner," that real change happened – for both of us.

Kiss My Curriculum

One day when my son was 13, he came into my bathroom as I was putting on makeup and said, "I look good!" Then he followed up with, "You look beautiful MOM!" Then he kissed me on the cheek and left with a huge smile on his face. One of my best Mommy moments.

That is when the whole lesson made sense to me. Here was this little boy who saw me as the most beautiful woman in his world. If I felt that the woman he saw was not worthy of praise, then how could he be worthy of praise? It was when I finally believed that I was beautiful that he allowed himself to feel the same about himself. What a God given gift!

By the way, all that mirror dancing and performing was full of lessons. After this experience I always kept a mirror in the main room of the house where all the kids, no matter how small, could see their reflection. As a result, all of our kids now love the stage. They are confident, whether speaking, singing, or acting. How grateful I am for their confidence, and. I believe that the mirror was a huge factor. That mirror was a miracle that I thought just entertained them. . Instead, it built confidence in an entire family. But, remember, confidence is copied first.

Kiss My Curriculum

"I was inspired by an amazing pack of worksheets in elementary school that totally changed my life!"

-Said No Child Ever

Lesson 6

Let Them Do It!

There is power in open creativity. Being given time, space, and means to create whatever you want is freeing. Every child needs to be able to feel that sense of accomplishment for themselves as early as possible, and as often as possible.

I learned a very powerful lesson when I worked with girls ages 12-18 at a week-long summer camp. Each year there was a different group of people making decisions. I saw a difference from year to year in the girls' attitudes depending on the control levels of the leaders.

Kiss My Curriculum

I saw this most distinctly in the art projects that were chosen for these youth to complete. Every year the leaders plan an art project for the girls to do during their free time. One of the first years I was a leader I had very little say in the planning as I was new and didn't yet have a voice yet. The art project that year was a small wooden picture frame that came in a neat little package. Once you took it out of the package, you put a stick in the back to hold it up, glued a wood flower on it, and painted it one of the five colors it came with. It was easy, clean, and could be completed quickly.

I watched as the girl's eyes clouded over when the art project came out. The leaders saw it as the natural rebellion of teenage girls and proceeded to try and get them excited about it. The girls displayed the emotions that were expected of them, did the project as prescribed, then went and took a nap. When it was time to pack up camp, I found a lot of painted wood frames no one would claim. Those frames were thrown away because no one cared.

Kiss My Curriculum

I remember the meeting when these picture frames were decided as the camp craft. I remember the leader talking about how wonderful this little art project would be. "It's all done for us," "There is very little mess," and "We won't have to do too much work for it!" These are some of the things said during the meeting. I remember being annoyed but I didn't know why.

Fast forward 10 years. I am now the leader in charge and it's time to plan the art activity. I have flashbacks of that first year, so I decided to try an experiment. I'm grateful I can, because I have more say in what happens. I suggest providing only supplies: stamps, markers, clay, paper of every kind, scissors, you name it. All of the leaders cleaned out our art supply cupboards and brought a little bit of everything.

I kept getting asked, "But what are they going to make?" I answered, "Who knows? Let's watch and see?" Some of the leaders looked at me like I was crazy. (I was used to this as an outside-the-box thinker.) But low and behold, that year was amazing!

Kiss My Curriculum

The girls did amazing things with their time, creativity, and supplies. They started leaving notes around for everyone. They decorated their tents and created jewelry. But mostly they created crafts for each other, their mothers, and their leaders. There was love in that camp like nothing I had ever seen.

We left the art supplies out throughout the duration of camp; we never took it down. The girls would get up early and stay up late talking and giggling while creating. Of course, we had few fights and breakdowns, but we also had girls who discovered they had artistic talent. They didn't have supplies at home, so they had never tried until they came to camp.

Was having all those supplies messy? OH YA! Was it expensive? A little, but a lot of leaders just brought old art supplies that weren't getting used at home. Regardless of the mess and the investment, it was totally worth it – in so many ways! We could have never predicted what all that art time would do for the camaraderie and stress in that camp. It made it all magical. Girls that normally wouldn't even talk to

Kiss My Curriculum

each other would sit side by side for hours chatting while creating and complimenting each other.

What is the lesson here? When a child or teen is given freedom and trust in opportunity and creativity, amazing things happen. Conversely, when a teen is told how to create and what to create, they feel demeaned and unvalued. That's when you get the rebellion. Luckily I got to learn this lesson on other people's teens while my kids were very young. I've remembered this lesson forever.

I find my teenagers are much more willing to work with me when they have a say in how things go. I see this easily in home decorating. That's something I've had to let go of in order to give them more space to create. When they care, I stand back and love whatever they come up with. Sometimes I don't love it, but I love that it comes from them. Now, I make it a point to get their opinions and help, even if I don't need it. I have found that it instills confidence in both of us. I see new ideas I would have never imagined, and they learn that their parents have faith in their abilities. They never cease to amaze me.

Kiss My Curriculum

Don't get me wrong, there have been some frustrating times when I would like to just do it myself and create what I want. I have often had to ask myself, "Don't I matter?" I remind myself that right now I matter to *them.* If I don't show my children that they can be creative and make beautiful things, who will? I am creating them (or more allowing them to create themselves) I find that allowing them to create themselves in their own way matters much more than where the painting should go or if the cake is decorated with the colors I want. Letting go is one of the hardest but one of the most important things I have learned to help our children find their creative selves. In so doing, we allow ourselves to be creative in new and exciting ways.

I am amazed at how many times adult pride not only gets in the way of youth progress, but actually stifles it. My kids have taught me that they don't need me or any adult to "tell them what to do." They want someone available to answer the questions they have, but they don't want someone to just give them answers – especially not answers to questions they don't have or haven't asked. These youth want a mentor to show them where to find the answers to the questions in their minds, to respect those ideas, and then help them to develop them. These youth are so much smarter than we give them credit for. They know what they want and what they need, and it's often not what we think they need and try to stuff into their brains.

My daughter had an experience recently where she was judged by the low expectations of the adults around her. We are very active in our church, and in the youth program, the youth are encouraged to teach a lesson to their peers. The lessons are intended to be interactive and non-lecture. They're supposed to be more of a discussion than a lesson.

One Sunday this daughter was assigned to give the lesson. She was so excited. She decided she was going to do it the way she wished to see a lesson done, so she coordinated the girls and had them ask questions about the topic (marriage) for the leaders to answer. She gathered the questions and asked each of the leaders if they would please answer them during class. Her goal was to get a discussion going based on the questions and the leader's answers.

One of the leaders responded to my daughter's request with, "If you don't want to prepare the lesson, we can give it to someone who wants it." She was crushed. And when another leader sent her a message that said, "The boys would like to combine our lessons. Since you haven't prepared anything anyway, I told them, 'yes,'" my daughter felt betrayed.

She said, "Mom, it's like they think that if I don't lecture and bring cookies and something tied with a ribbon, then it can't be a lesson." Then she said, "Can I come to the adult class with you? The youth program is getting in the way of my testimony." She just wanted to be given the chance to try something new and show she could make a meaningful lesson.

It can be so hard to trust the instincts of our children and let them explore their creativity when they are young, but it pays off in large numbers when they are teens. So how can parents let children explore their creativity when they are young, when it matters most?

I can tell you one way that can hinder creativity: extracurricular activities. Like most parents in this century, we were sucked into the idea that we needed to start our children young in a sport or music lesson if we wanted them to be great at it when they were older. Luckily we couldn't afford much when they were young.

We started small with sports through the community and piano from a neighbor. We quickly realized that our kids although interested at first, lost interest quickly in the sport of instrument because the coach was mean or pushy, or the music teachers would be overly strict. The kids preferred to play at home together instead of going to lessons. I found myself fighting them for lessons they didn't want and we couldn't really afford.

So I stopped fighting them on the different lessons I thought they needed. I decided that the kids could have a lesson that they wanted once they could come to me and ask for it, but that I wouldn't offer anymore. It just got too hard and expensive.

I worried that once they were interested in something, they would be too far behind the other kids and not able to keep up. However, once my kids were high school age and started asking for music lessons, something interesting happened. They picked their lessons, guitar, piano, drums, and worked on without any help from me. No convincing, no prodding. If they liked it, they took off. If they didn't like it, then they let it go and looked for something else.

I stopped getting upset over their need to try something and started seeing it as a natural aspect of childhood, because it is. Each instrument or class led them to learn more about themselves. There were some skills they stuck to and really developed, while there were others they would take for a while, discover an aspect of themselves, but ultimately chose to go in a different direction.

The most important thing I learned was that if I waited for them to ask me for the class, then they dedicated themselves to it. We would work out some sort of deal for them to do for me so that I could put in the money or time for their lesson and they work hard without me having to get after them. Giving my teens this freedom has allowed them to pick what they want out of life. It's probably been more expensive for us this way, but I've learned that trusting their interests and their abilities to decide their interests for themselves has brought them great confidence.

This all ties back to failure. Allowing our children to explore their creativity in this unique way emphasized that they didn't fail at a class or skill; they just weren't as interested as they thought they were. Once again, they just don't see failure at all. This opens up a world of freedom to discover who they are, without judgement from us.

Kiss My Curriculum

"When you Homeschool the world is your classroom. Science is optional."

Lesson 7

Illness and Trials are Wonderful Homeschool Lessons

As homeschool parents, we have lived with a lot of doubt and guilt. "What if it's not enough?" "What if we ruin them?" " What if we don't have them sufficiently prepared for the real world?" All parents carry doubts; however, it seems homeschool parents have a bigger bag of them. Looking back after 16 years, I see that their education is not at all what I thought it would be; it's better. We asked God to help us raise these kids, and he is raising them. Thank goodness he is a wise parent and Master teacher.

Kiss My Curriculum

One of the ways God helped raise our children was through illnesses. Sickness is a beautiful teacher. One winter when our kids were newborn to almost 10 years old, each of them got hand, foot, and mouth disease. One at a time their mouths started showing sores, then their hands, and finally their feet. Of course, they didn't get it the same day. Hand, foot and mouth disease is a 10-day illness, so when they each get it days apart, it becomes a whole month of illness.

We made beds for all of the kids in the living room so that we would not be running all over the house. We moved the TV from the downstairs family room upstairs living room right off the kitchen so that I could be nearby at all times. During this time, of course, all "formal" learning stopped. It was around the clock medicines, ice cream, cold drinks, you name it. Once all 5 had it, I felt a bit desperate. So we came together as a family knelt down and asked for help.

What happened that month was beautiful. I watched as my children had patience with each other. I watched as each child had compassion on others and helped wherever they could. We went through a lot of movies, which made me feel like a failure because they were getting absolutely no lessons. I thought I was rotting our brains out. But once it was all over, I could see how sweet that month really was. God put a feeling of peace in our house that was different than we had experienced before.

We had to cut out everything. My husband had to cancel all of his meetings. No one came over, and we didn't leave for anything but groceries. And it turned out to be heavenly. All the kids were crammed into one small space cuddled up. I sat in the middle of them for hours just holding one, then another. It was magical.

We learned a lot that month, even without the formal lessons. We learned that sometimes it's important to shut out the world and just enjoy each other. We learned that the illness is sometimes the lesson. My kids learned how to take care of each other, including how to take a temperature, a practical skill, and how to comfort, a skill of the heart. They learned how to be patient in affliction, that suffering together was better than suffering alone, and they saw how much we as parents sacrifice for them. The older kids could see how hard this was on mom and dad, and they were so grateful and kind.

We have had many "family illnesses" since. We have come to look forward to them. Twisted I know. But now if I see a flu coming on, I head to the store, load up on the food items we'll want, and get ready for the family downtime. Though our bodies are ill, our spirits are the ones that heal. Every time this happens, we don't just heal physically, we heal emotionally as well. We often don't even know we need emotional healing, but HE does.

When our kids were between the ages of 5-16 a new phenomenon entered our life: Dad traveling consistently. We moved from our home in Maryland to Utah where we could be near our families. Dad stayed with NASA, and they let him work from home part time. When we first moved, he had to go back East every month for two weeks. Slowly, over five years, the traveling became less and less, allowing more time at home, but until then, it was rough.

Kiss My Curriculum

Homeschooling was rough, but those illnesses were even harder while Dad was out of town. It didn't matter when the illnesses came, they were guaranteed to happen while Dad was out of town. Especially if I got sick too, and this was a time when I started getting sick frequently. I had been extremely healthy up to this point, but all of a sudden I was picking up every stomach flu, cold, horrible bug, whatever came around. I was often first to get it, Then as I was recovering, the kids would each work their way through it as well. I was extremely grateful to have gotten it first so that I could be more compassionate towards their symptoms. (I am usually a "suck it up" kind of gal.)

After several years of only getting sick while my husband was gone and spending days on a couch unable to take care of my kids, I cried out to God in utter frustration and asked, "Why would you do this to us?! I am trying my best to be a good mom, and you take not only my health but my husband as well! What is going on?" (This was a particularly rough stomach flu.)

Kiss My Curriculum

I am so grateful for the Lord's patience in our suffering and whining. His answer was simple, again. "Watch what is happening while you are sick. See not what you can't do, but what THEY can."

My eyes were opened and I noticed that while I was laying on the couch, my children were taking care of each other. My older kids made meals and cleaned up; they entertained the younger ones and kept them quiet while I slept. They checked on me, covered me with blankets, and brought me water and tissues. They were learning how to take care of each other, but most importantly they were learning to take care of me.

As parents we don't think of that as an important lesson. It is our job to be the caregivers, right? But our kids learned that I was breakable and that mothers also need care. They learned that when they are parents, there will be rough days, and that's okay. We are in this together, as a family; We take care of each other. They learned that they have the power to strengthen the adult; I didn't just exist for them but them for us as well.

Kiss My Curriculum

This was a new kind of lesson. I learned that it is ok to need help from your kids, no matter what the age. They learned that they are needed. Kids need to be needed, and taking care of mom made them feel capable, confident, and needed. My husband is a very loving kind person who would have taken care of all of us beautifully, but God removed his loving care so that our kids could discover that they have loving care to give and their contribution was vital to the life of the family.

We have recently learned this lesson again. We never seem to learn a lesson after only one time. Thank goodness that God has the wisdom to reteach us when we need it. My husband and I had experienced a rough 4 years. We had some business ideas that went bad and ended up in financial stress, then my husband broke his leg and ended up with a very expensive surgery (14 pins and a rod in his leg), we lost family and friends, appliances and cars broke down – you name it. It got to the point where we would jokingly get up in the morning (trying not to cry), and prepare ourselves for the next bad news. It was rough on our marriage, our kids, and our health.

As the pressure started to lift, our health took a dive, mine in particular. My adrenal glands were shot. My body stopped functioning, and I ended up on the couch for months. Once again it felt like a punishment. But not being able to be the Energizer Bunny, helped me see my world differently. As I had no physical energy but was still functioning mentally, I started noticing some things in my kids that I had been too "busy" to see before.

I realized that my oldest was sleeping a lot. Yes, she was a teen, but it seemed a bit extreme. I took her to the doctor to find out she was dangerously anemic; we got her stable. My second oldest was having a lot of weird pains. I got her to a chiropractor and found that she, too, had some issues that needed my attention, including some anemia and low progesterone. My third child was healthy, but his writing was suffering. He was now in school but struggling because he was embarrassed by his writing skills, and he was also failing a class. I started working with him daily again; it had been awhile.

My fourth child was really tired and seemed to always get sick. After she climbed into bed with me one night after yet another nightmare, I noticed her loud snoring. She and her little brother needed their tonsils out, so we had them removed. Now they are happier without nightmares. My youngest child was not reading as well as a 7-year-old should be. So, I got back to reading with him. I didn't even realize I had stopped.

Thank goodness my health tanked or I am not sure that I would have seen the needs of my kids so clearly. I realized how much I had been lost in our financial and grown up problems, and how much I had missed about my children. I was not truly seeing them, though they were right in front of me. Illness is so hard! But I believe its purpose is to teach us the most important lessons in life: That family is everything, that God loves us, and that we are in this together.

Kiss My Curriculum

It wasn't always sicknesses that taught us important lessons but trials and tragedies as well.

One of those trials came when my kids were between the ages of 4 and 15. The three-year-old son of dear friends was hit by a car just in front of our house. This little boy was dear to our hearts. I was the organizational leader of the women of my church at that time, which meant I was one of the first to get the call. My husband was out of town and I was in the middle of homeschooling my kids when I had to drop everything and get to the ER. I was gone for hours comforting my dear friends as their precious child passed into the next life.

As one of the main leaders, I was called upon constantly for the next several weeks. First I assisted in planning the funeral, then I orchestrated food and order as hundreds came to pay their respect to this family. Needless to say, the neighborhood was hurting and so many friends, neighbors and family members were calling me to ask how they could help this beloved family.

Kiss My Curriculum

We came up with a plan. We conspired with the neighborhood and their extended family to fix up their house while the extended family got the grieving family out of town. We had one week to make miracles. As a neighborhood, we deep cleaned the house, had the carpets and furniture cleaned, fixed gutters, planted flowers and cleaned up the yard, and fixed or replaced everything that was broken. One neighbor came and remodeled a bathroom that was only partly functional. It was a beautiful and sad time for us all.

My kids were older during this tragedy, and they had loved this little boy and love his family. While everyone else's kids went back to school to grieve our kids jumped right in to help out. My older girls took care of the younger kids, served food at the funeral, and cleaned up afterwards. They helped to clean the house, and they worked and worked right alongside me as we did our best to comfort hundreds. They helped the family with small chores as they started their healing process. This time they didn't play as the adults worked, they got their hands dirty, and sacrificed for others. I believe the opportunity to be there to help in a time of need, helped our children to heal as well. It was truly a bittersweet time of love and service for our family.

Even though the event was tragic and changed all of our lives forever, we learned to work together as a family. We cried together, laughed together, and served together. When did we teach these skills and attributes? They learned it through watching us their whole lives while we struggled through other trials. We just didn't know it. We always felt that we were in everything together and tried to explain what was happening best as we could so they would understand. We always allowed them to help wherever possible and never sent them to be watched while we dealt with a problem. We counted on them, even at young ages, to help out and be a part of the family. So now when tragedy strikes they look at us and say, "How can I help?" They now know what to do, with confidence, when trials and tragedies come along. It is times like these that heaven smiles down on us and says "your welcome".

Kiss My Curriculum

I am so grateful that our children have had the opportunity to experience all these things at our feet, instead of on their own as adults, possibly thousands of miles away from us. They experienced these things while we were near and could guide them, working alongside them, and show them that even with four inches of water in your basement, no electricity for a week, and other neighbors in need, we could work together happily and lighten loads. We have learned to be happy during the trying times because we could find the silver lining in it together. I am grateful that they learned that tragedy does not break us but make us stronger.

Kiss My Curriculum

"Curiosity + Creativity = Confidence"

Lesson 8

Curious, Creative and Confident, Blessing? Or Curse?

Creativity's Destroyers

We value our children's creativity and have found that it must be protected carefully. All kids have amazing imaginations, but imaginations are easily destroyed by fear. We were surprised to find that one of the ways fear snuck into our house was through media, specifically movies. We have always been careful with movies and other media that might make our children's imaginations run a little wild, but

Kiss My Curriculum

we were surprised when a simple movie like Disney's The Lion King could inspire so much negative imaginations.

After watching the Lion King our daughter was having nightmares of her Daddy dying. She dreamt of lions and hyenas eating her. She saw evil for the first time and was scared for weeks. We didn't sleep because of her sensitivities to this. It took her years before she was even able to hear Mufasa's song without shivering. All of our children have followed suit. Recently my 10-year-old daughter had a nightmare about a poorly-done Halloween junior high play and my 16-year-old cried after seeing "The Prestige".

We don't believe that movies in and of themselves destroy creativity, but a creative mind can take an idea given by a movie and distort it into fear. We've learned to be even more careful of all movies we let into our home. Sure, it puts a damper on movie night, but our kids have stayed sensitive, which has kept their creativity so pure and powerful. I have also watched movies enhance their creativity. They reenact their favorite scenes, try out new ideas, sing along or get inspired by a story. It's about choosing inspiring movies verses something that could scare them or be too intense for their minds. Being careful of the movies they watch keeps them sensitive to the world around them. We are careful not to desensitize them.

I've learned that growing creativity in my children means letting them be themselves, even when I don't really want them to be. Sometimes I just really want them to do it my way. It would be so much easier. But doing it my way doesn't expand their creative natures.

For example, we love coloring. We often get out coloring books while Dad reads to us. I would open up a fresh box of crayons or markers, get out a book, carefully pick a page that I was excited to color and begin. (I find coloring very relaxing). It is never long before one of the kids comes and sits on my lap and says, "Let's color this page together." I let them and they proceed to pick a color that clashes with my preconceived ideas for my masterpiece. They would color the one section I really didn't want colored, then lose interest, put the marker back in the wrong place, and go play.

I am actually having a bit of anxiety as I write this. It was so hard to let them choose and let them color. Luckily I knew to keep my mouth shut, tell them I loved their help, but inside I was annoyed that I couldn't finish the paper the way I wanted it. Sometimes I just wanted something that didn't have a "child mark" on it.

By my last few kids, I started to realize that if I pushed them away, I was teaching them that I didn't want them around and that their opinions didn't matter. I remember hearing the soft whisper say things like, "If you want teens to value your opinion, then value their opinions as toddlers." "Let them team up with you now and they always will." Boy am I grateful for those little inspirations, and I am so grateful I kept my mouth shut all those years and never let them know their help kind of drove me crazy. I didn't know that biting my tongue, holding them on my lap and letting them just do as they wanted would be such a big thing as they got older.

Now they know they are always welcome to help or have an opinion of one of my projects, and they come willing to help. They offer great insights, and my projects are now better because of their opinions and help. I enjoy them more when they have suggestions and offer help. I wonder if they would be so willing to help me now if I had sent them away during coloring time when they were little. I am not sure, but I am glad I listened to that wonderful whisper. It took 15 years before I got to finish an entire coloring page by myself. But now I look at my finished piece and miss that there is no little opinion added to it.

Let Go of Perfection. Let Go of Control.

I often find that I want my children's masterpieces to turn out beautiful and perfect. I've struggled letting them express their creativity in their own unique ways, but when I let go of that control, my children thrive. They always amaze me with their creations.

A great example of this happened Halloween 2019. Every Halloween my mother throws an amazing costume party. She plans for it all year, and my kids look forward to it. Each party is themed (Harry Potter, Star Wars, Minions, Monsters Inc, You name it). And while my mother does an amazing job, each of my kids wants their own extravagant costume. My kids are extremely creative and think big. They start early and plan out what they want to do, and sometimes supporting five different imaginations and ideas is rough. We have fed our children's independence and creativeness, but this Halloween party is the test of my beliefs in these concepts and my endurance.

Halloween 2019 was themed after "How to Train Your Dragon." I, of course, think, "Great. I will get on Pinterest and look up some dragon masks, we will get some felt to make masks, wear some colored shirts, and we are done."

Kiss My Curriculum

My kids had their own ideas

I take all the kids to JoAnne's to get the material needed for their ideas. We come up with new ideas while looking at the fabric, but they wouldn't have it. Everyone left frustrated and some were even in tears because I kept bringing up new ideas of things we could do and they didn't like it.

Not one of my ideas were used.

Children 1 and 2 decided to be Toughnut and Roughnut. The twins. I had no idea how to do that. Luckily they were old enough to get started on their own. They asked for yarn to make a wig and felt to make the rest. I had no idea how they were going to do that but I figured they were on their own. They turned out some amazing costumes and taught me a thing or two about how to be creative with little.

Child #3 decided to make Toothless out of cardboard boxes that he could get in and out of. He wanted the wings to contract and expand. He needed, boxes, chicken wire, duct tape, spray paint, a mask, etc. etc. His list was a mile long. Once again I thought, "He is 13; he is on his own." I got him his stuff, and he worked for weeks. I kept asking if he needed help, but he kept turning me down. He ended up giving up on his idea the day of the party with a costume ¾ of the way done because he refused to accept ideas or help from anyone.

Child #4 wanted to be a two-headed dragon. I had no idea how to make a two-headed dragon, so I tried to convince her for weeks that she wanted to be something I knew how to make. She refused. I threw my hands up in frustration and said, "Fine but you are going to have to do it yourself." That 10-year-old made an adorable sock puppet for one head, asked her sister for some clothes, and made a felt mask for the other head that she wore. She is 10! I have to admit I was pleasantly surprised with what she came up with, never discouraged at her mother's need to control. She just kept letting me know that she had it under control, and she did.

Child #5 had his own idea all together. He will not be controlled, but he is the baby, so I had hoped to have some say in an adorable costume for him.

Kiss My Curriculum

Nope. He had something very specific in mind. when we were at JoAnne's, he took his older sister to the fabric and showed her what he wanted (I think he knew I was trying to choose for him). He wanted a mermaid blue sparkly fabric to be his wings and another color to be the tail. So we bought it, and all I could think was, "this is not going to work."

But they proved me wrong. My daughter cut out his wings and tail to his specifications and figured out how to make them work. He had me help him with a mask. I carefully cut out a toothless mask and made it look just like him, but child #5 wanted to add his own touches to it, which consisted of him cutting out different colors of material and sticking it all over my carefully made mask. I had to walk away. His final costume was made by a 7-year-old and a 16-year-old. It did not look like a professionally put together costume.

In fact, not one costume for that party looked professional. They would probably not get any pins on Pinterest for their creativity. I for sure will not get mom of the year because of their costumes. It was hard not to control it all, but what happened when they had control was amazing. My kids worked together (most of them) to create a vision in their heads. When they were done they were proud of their work. This gave them confidence in their own abilities to create something out of nothing. When they showed up at the party, they arrived with cousins who had bought their costumes on Amazon, but they weren't ashamed like I expected. They were thrilled with what they had made. It actually made them even more proud of what they had accomplished. When we got home they put it in the costume box for another costume later.

I learned that when it is hardest for me to let go, it is the most important time to do so. I also learned that they don't care about Pinterest and neither should I. I think I will make our own Family Pinterest board with all that they have done. Regardless of the opinion of the world.

Kiss My Curriculum

Confidence in Creativity

Letting our children develop their individual creativity has developed their confidence. I love this. It is so rewarding to see our children express their opinions and creations with confidence. However, our children have embarrassed us on more than one occasion. I guess we have pushed free thought so much that it is often confused for rebellion by other adults. And it may be a little bit of rebellion (they get that from me).

Last fall, I was at a painting activity with several other women in my neighborhood. I asked if my 15-year-old would like to come. She heartily agreed; she loves painting. We were sitting around painting wood cutouts of monsters for Halloween when she joins us at the table and asks in a very loud voice if she can see the project and what the samples look like so that she knows what not to do. I am mortified. These are my friends, and I am afraid she has offended them especially since, obviously her mother was to blame for her behavior.

Kiss My Curriculum

Here's the truth: I have taught her that the only rules that she must follow are God's rules and the law of the land. Everything else she needs to check for herself and decide if it is a good rule or a bad rule. Follow good rules; help to make a difference for the bad rules – that is more or less our philosophy.

I may have neglected to go over what is polite when deciding which rules NOT to follow. I'll work on that.

All that said, I am all for not being told what to do when it comes to an art project. I figure, what is the point of an art project that doesn't allow for creativity? I think I may have taken it too far. I think I forgot the lesson about being yourself *without* offending others intentionally. That night, I nudged her to try and signal to her that she needs to keep her natural rebellion under wrap unless she wants to offend the creator of the project.

Instead, after I nudged her, she said proudly, "But Mom, you're the one who taught me not to follow instructions!" Wow, did that lesson get misconstrued. It's not like I could explain right then and there that we believe that our kids should not wait to be instructed in all things and that they needed to think for themselves, not follow blindly.

We often tell our children that we did not give birth to Lemmings. That lesson seems to have sunk in. However, when and where to show that individual spirit is something we are still working on. And unfortunately for us, it is always at the worst times that they decide to test those ideas. Time to go over how to apply your questioning spirit. By the way, the project she painted was adorable and original. So at least we got that lesson right.

Creative Conflicts: Holidays

Holidays are another time that having creative thinkers is a real pain in the butt. Here is why. I want all of my kids to have an opinion on how we decorate because I want everyone to feel a part of the holidays. They live in this house too, and we want them to be proud of the area they live in. It's all great – in theory.

Kiss My Curriculum

Every year I imagine a day where we turn on Christmas music, get out snacks, and decorate the tree together while we have a magical evening as a family. Every year it goes more like this: We use the plastic tree in one room where Dad can decorate it without little hands and opinions. We give him all the breakable stuff, and he decorates a very elegant tree. Mom has to have a fresh one, so the kids help me pick out one that has "personality." We name it, (doesn't everyone?), then bring it home and discuss its personality and how it needs to be decorated. We never agree. When six people all have designs of their own in their heads, fights ensue.

To make holiday decorating more pleasant, we divide up the whole house. Everyone gets a section that they get to decorate according to their liking. No one else is allowed to have an opinion or go in behind them and change anything. This has helped keep the peace a bit more, but it has also caused Mom and Dad a lot of frustration. Especially when the boys have devilish ideas of underwear on trees, mismatched decor, and such. I am convinced they do it just to bother their sisters' more artistic interests. Some years it has become almost territorial as each claims their decorating spot to either outdo the other or drive others crazy. We have one daughter who is a perfectionist. Another one of our children is the opposite. So their decorating zones drive each other crazy the whole season.

Our dream of "Hey let's decorate the house for Christmas with a feeling of peace and unity" is a bunch of bunk! But our house is always interesting, and every year either my husband or I will be heard saying, "The day we can do it the way we want will be a sad day."

Yes, creative, intelligent, curious, confident children can be a real pain when they don't see the world our way. But if they did, they wouldn't open our minds and hearts in ways we never could have imagined. These creative, intelligent, curious, and confident children teach us how to treat others, follow the spirit, and occasionally call us to repentance. They help us to be better, because they rarely agree with us. It is humbling. It is wonderful!

Kiss My Curriculum

Final Thoughts

Homeschooling was not my first choice. I fought it with tooth and nail at first. But I have been homeschooled throughout the process. I have learned more history, science, writing and math then I ever learned as a kid. I have learned that I am capable, intelligent, and creative.

Homeschooling my children has taught me how to teach myself whatever I want and not sit and mourn over a lost degree. It is knowledge that I now seek and that I teach my children to seek. If a degree comes out of it then so be it.

I have learned that my limits are only in my own mind. That I can accomplish anything I want. My kids have taught me all this. Either through them or because of them.

I am eternally grateful for this opportunity to be a homeschool parent. To have my children around me their whole lives. I am blessed to have my kids my best friends. I am grateful for a Heavenly

Kiss My Curriculum

Father who loves me and my kids, who is very interested in all of our well-being. I love the way he taught us to work together, serve together, and suffer together. In the end no matter what happens in my children's lives, I will know, I gave everything for their well-being. But I received so much more in return.

Rebecca Strömsdörfer originated, wrote, and published her book – Kiss My Curriculum – using an online program through Mangobelly.com. The course uses the same format used by best sellers and is offered 100 percent online. It walks from idea creation to published product with additional personal coaching offers as needed. To learn more, go to Mangobelly.com (online courses) and use the discount code, REBECCA199, for a special discount.

(This is not a paid advertisement)

About the Author

Rebecca is first and foremost a wife and mother – these are her favorite roles and greatest accomplishments. Nothing brings her greater joy than being with her husband and children.

She was a reluctant homeschooler 17 years ago. Forced into homeschooling because of the area they lived in, she had to go at it alone. Now 17 years and a lot of experience later she believes it is the best thing she has ever done for her kids, herself, and her family.

She is co-owner of "Messy Perfection Homeschooling" on Facebook and Instagram. She dedicates her life to helping new homeschoolers relax and enjoy the journey. She is also in constant motion starting new programs for teens to help them fill their hunger for learning, so that they can meet their potential. She is wife to her best friend, and mother to 5.

When she's not being a wife and mom, Rebecca loves to pursue her vast interests: finance, business, homeschooling, and education. She's currently working on a project to combine all of her interests to bless even more lives.

Rebecca is just getting started, but stay-tuned for more innovative approaches to education, business, and homeschooling. Follow her at:

https://www.facebook.com/groups/3038399233052904/
https://www.instagram.com/messyperfectionhomeschooler/
https://MPHomeschooler.com

Made in United States
North Haven, CT
15 April 2023

35488994R00074